The
Garden

by Sara Kwan

illustrated by Amy Loeffler

PEARSON

Scott
Foresman

Editorial Offices: Glenview, Illinois • Parsippany, New Jersey • New York, New York
Sales Offices: Needham, Massachusetts • Duluth, Georgia • Glenview, Illinois
Coppell, Texas • Sacramento, California • Mesa, Arizona

Every effort has been made to secure permission and provide appropriate credit for photographic material. The publisher deeply regrets any omission and pledges to correct errors called to its attention in subsequent editions.

Unless otherwise acknowledged, all photographs are the property of Scott Foresman, a division of Pearson Education.

Photo locators denoted as follows: Top (T), Center (C), Bottom (B), Left (L), Right (R), Background (Bkgd)

Illustrations by Amy Loeffler

Photograph 8 ©DK Images

ISBN: 0-328-13187-3

7 8 9 10 V010 14 13 12 11 10 09 08

"I'm afraid our lesson has ended,"
said Mr. Murk.
"But we will start something new again.
How can we find out about plants?"

"We can read and plant a garden,"
said Barb.
The class said it was a good plan.
Soon they got started.

"Let's draw our garden," said Carl.
The class said it was a good plan.
Soon they got started.

"Let's start digging and plant the seeds,"
said Kirk.
The class said it was a good plan.
Soon they got started.

A few weeks passed.
"Let's pick our vegetables," said Barb.
The class said it was a good plan.
It was a very good plan.

Growing and Changing

Read Together

Like other living things, green plants grow and change. Many plants begin as a seed. Seeds need water, the right kind of soil, and the right temperature to grow. If seeds get what they need, roots will grow down to hold the plant in place. The roots get water and food from the soil. A stem grows up toward the sun. Soon leaves will grow from the stem. They will use light from the sun to make food for the plant.